An Animal Family
RABBITS AND KITS

By Natalie Humphrey

Gareth Stevens
PUBLISHING

Please visit our website, www.garethstevens.com. For a free color catalog of all our high-quality books, call toll free 1-800-542-2595 or fax 1-877-542-2596.

Library of Congress Cataloging-in-Publication Data

Names: Humphrey, Natalie, author.
Title: Rabbits and kits / Natalie Humphrey.
Description: New York : Gareth Stevens Publishing, [2021] | Series: An
    animal family | Includes index.
Identifiers: LCCN 2019045217 | ISBN 9781538255841 (library binding) | ISBN
    9781538255827 (paperback) | ISBN 9781538255834 (6 Pack) | ISBN 9781538255858
    (ebook)
Subjects: LCSH: Rabbits–Infancy–Juvenile literature. |
    Rabbits–Development–Juvenile literature.
Classification: LCC QL737.L32 H86 2021 | DDC 599.3213/92–dc23
LC record available at https://lccn.loc.gov/2019045217

First Edition

Published in 2021 by
Gareth Stevens Publishing
111 East 14th Street, Suite 349
New York, NY 10003

Editor: Natalie Humphrey
Designer: Katelyn E. Reynolds

Photo credits: Cover, p. 1 Victoria Antonova/Shutterstock.com; p. 5 PACO COMO/Shutterstock.com; pp. 7, 24 (fur) Andrea Coughlin/EyeEm/Getty Images; pp. 9, 24 (nest) Jim Larkin/Shutterstock.com; pp. 11, 24 (twig) Alexey Stiop/Shutterstock.com; p. 13 Anikakodydkova/Shutterstock.com; p. 15 Real Moment/Shutterstock.com; p. 17 OlhaSemeniv/Shutterstock.com; p. 19 © iStockphoto.com/Me-che; p. 21 Nick Biemans/Shutterstock.com; p. 23 MANAT23/Shutterstock.com.

Printed in the United States of America

Some of the images in this book illustrate individuals who are models. The depictions do not imply actual situations or events.

CPSIA compliance information: Batch #CS20GS: For further information contact Gareth Stevens, New York, New York at 1-800-542-2595.

Find us on

Contents

Safe at Home. 4

Lots of Babies. 12

Growing up Fast 20

Words to Know 24

Index. 24

A kit is a baby rabbit.

Mother rabbits
build nests.
They are made of
fur and twigs.

Baby rabbits stay in
the nest.
Mothers hide them.

This keeps them safe!

Mothers have
6 to 14 kits.

Mothers leave during
the day.
They eat far away from
the nest.

They eat plants.
They return to feed
their kits.

Mothers make milk.
Kits drink it.

Kits grow up fast!

It can take only
four weeks.

Words to Know

fur   nest   twig

Index

grow up 20   mother 6, 8,
milk 18   12, 14, 18

24